D0101970

THE
EMERGENCY
POET

The Emergency Poet was conceived by poet and writer Deborah Alma as a fun way of bringing poetry to people.

A mix of the serious, the therapeutic and the theatrical, the Emergency Poet offers consultations inside her vintage ambulance and prescribes poems as cures.

Dressed in white coat and stethoscope, and accompanied by Nurse Verse or a Poemedic, she travels to literary and music festivals, libraries, schools, pubs, weddings and conferences.

Deborah also works with poetry to help communicate with people with dementia and at the end of their lives, and teaches Writing Poetry at the University of Worcester.

She has a BA in Creative Writing from the University of Birmingham and an MA in Creative Writing from Keele University.

THE
EMERGENCY
POET

An Anti-Stress
Poetry Anthology

EDITED BY
Deborah Alma

Michael O'Mara Books Limited

First published in Great Britain in 2015 by
Michael O'Mara Books Limited
9 Lion Yard
Tremadoc Road
London SW4 7NQ

Every reasonable effort has been made to acknowledge all
copyright holders. Any errors or omissions that may have
occurred are inadvertent, and anyone with any copyright queries
is invited to write to the publisher, so that a full acknowledgement
may be included in subsequent editions of this work.

A CIP catalogue record for this book is available from the
British Library.

Papers used by Michael O'Mara Books Limited are natural,
recyclable products made from wood grown in sustainable forests.
The manufacturing processes conform to the environmental
regulations of the country of origin.

ISBN: 978-1-78243-405-4 in hardback print format

5 7 9 10 8 6 4

Designed and typeset by www.glensaville.com

Printed and bound by CPI Group (UK) Ltd, Croydon, CR0 4YY

www.mombooks.com

CONTENTS

Over the land freckled with snow half-thawed
The speculating rooks at their nests cawed
And saw from elm-tops, delicate as flowers of grass,
What we below could not see, Winter pass.

– EDWARD THOMAS

Introduction

I grew up on a North London council estate where poetry, if it was ever considered at all, was thought of as 'poncy'; it was something for intellectual types, something you had to study at school, something difficult. It was certainly not for the likes of us.

Years later, the council estate girl bought a 1970s ambulance from eBay and took poetry out to people who were frightened of it, put it in their hands and said, 'Yes, it is for you. This one is especially for you!'

The poems I have prescribed in these pages are all tried and tested – certain to offer empathy, guidance and relieve stress. They have been given to people in hospitals and care homes, at events at libraries and schools, and to people at festivals and in town centres who have wandered into the back of my old ambulance for a little poetry therapy and gentle conversation. Often looking for counsel and an emotional pick-me-up, they find verses to lift the spirits, to console and to help cope with all of the pressures of the modern day.

I have organized the poems into sections that follow a life through its challenges and hard times: from learning to be yourself, falling in and out of love and having children, through to ill-health, dying and coping with grief, as well as a few poems that serve as tonics to lift the spirits.

Some of the poems cover more than one emotional need, so cast around: you may find something that also applies to you in a different chapter. Dip in and use them as and when you need that emotional release. (I have also listed other poems at the end of the book as further reading that I would have liked to include if I had had the space.)

Take a look for yourself. The poems speak intimately as though from one person to another, and with intelligence, wisdom and accessibility; like a good friend over a kitchen table. Let the rhythms in the verses soothe you; learn the poem that speaks to you, recite it in your head. Make it yours. Take a moment with a glass of wine, a pot of tea or a hot chocolate and sit out in the sunshine or by the fire; give the poems some time and they will give back to you over and over again.

FOR DAYS WHEN THE WORLD IS TOO MUCH WITH US ...

There are those days when life is all too much: when work is taking over our lives, when it's hard to get out of bed in the morning or when, as tired as you are, you still can't sleep.

The poems in this chapter remind us to stop, even if it's for only a moment, and put things in perspective. Focus on the essential, best parts of life: of love, friends and family; the simple pleasure of being able to 'sit out in the sun and listen'. The beautiful poem 'Postscript' by Seamus Heaney reminds us that it is only when we take the time to stand in an in-between place, between the calm lake and the stormy sea, that we can have the space to welcome in change and all of its possibilities.

The Peace of Wild Things

WENDELL BERRY

When despair for the world grows in me
and I wake in the night at the least sound
in fear of what my life and my children's lives may be,
I go and lie down where the wood drake
rests in his beauty on the water, and the great heron
    feeds.
I come into the peace of wild things
who do not tax their lives with forethought
of grief. I come into the presence of still water.
And I feel above me the day-blind stars
waiting with their light. For a time
I rest in the grace of the world, and am free.

Inessential Things

BRIAN PATTEN

What do cats remember of days?

They remember the ways in from the cold,
the warmest spot, the place of food.
They remember the places of pain, their enemies,
the irritation of birds, the warm fumes of the soil,
the usefulness of dust.
They remember the creak of a bed, the sound
of their owner's footsteps,
the taste of fish, the loveliness of cream.
Cats remember what is essential of days.
Letting all other memories go as of no worth
they sleep sounder than we,
whose hearts break remembering so many
inessential things.

The Word

TONY HOAGLAND

Down near the bottom
of the crossed-out list
of things you have to do today,

between 'green thread'
and 'broccoli' you find
that you have penciled 'sunlight'.

Resting on the page, the word
is beautiful. It touches you
as if you had a friend

and sunlight were a present
he had sent from someplace distant
as this morning – to cheer you up,

and to remind you that,
among your duties, pleasure
is a thing

that also needs accomplishing.
Do you remember?
that time and light are kinds

of love, and love
is no less practical
than a coffee grinder

or a safe spare tire?
Tomorrow you may be utterly
without a clue,

but today you get a telegram
from the heart in exile,
proclaiming that the kingdom

still exists,
the king and queen alive,
still speaking to their children,

– to any one among them
who can find the time
to sit out in the sun and listen.

The Lake Isle of Innisfree

WILLIAM BUTLER YEATS

I will arise and go now, and go to Innisfree,
And a small cabin build there, of clay and wattles made;
Nine bean rows will I have there, a hive for the honey bee,
    And live alone in the bee-loud glade.
And I shall have some peace there, for peace comes
    dropping slow,
Dropping from the veils of the morning to where the
    cricket sings;
There midnight's all a glimmer, and noon a purple glow,
    And evening full of the linnet's wings.

I will arise and go now, for always night and day
I hear lake water lapping with low sounds by the shore;
While I stand on the roadway, or on the pavements grey,
    I hear it in the deep heart's core.

Leisure

W. H. DAVIES

What is this life if, full of care,
We have no time to stand and stare.

No time to stand beneath the boughs
And stare as long as sheep or cows.

No time to see, when woods we pass,
Where squirrels hide their nuts in grass.

No time to see, in broad daylight,
Streams full of stars, like skies at night.

No time to turn at Beauty's glance,
And watch her feet, how they can dance.

No time to wait till her mouth can
Enrich that smile her eyes began.

A poor life this is if, full of care,
We have no time to stand and stare.

Pax

D. H. LAWRENCE

All that matters is to be at one with the living God
to be a creature in the house of the God of Life.

Like a cat asleep on a chair
at peace, in peace
and at one with the master of the house, with the
    mistress,
at home, at home in the house of the living,
sleeping on the hearth, and yawning before the fire.

Sleeping on the hearth of the living world
yawning at home before the fire of life
feeling the presence of the living God
like a great reassurance
a deep calm in the heart
a presence
as of a master sitting at the board
in his own and greater being,
in the house of life.

Insomnia has had a very bad press

CHAR MARCH

but, imagine yourself
a large, grey seal:
bob up for air
rise and fall with the swell
of deep-night
when all sounds
are strange, distorted,
and your whiskered snout
radars through fug and fog.

now dive into shallow
then deeper sleep,
turn your dappled belly up
wave a flipper
at a shoal of passing thoughts
snooze for a brief dream
of mackerel,
then rise in a stream of bubbles
to take the air again.

Awake at Night

MEG COX

and listening to the World Service
(one benefit of sleeping on my own)
I heard a man explain he wasn't lonely;
he talked to his dead wife all the time
although he knew she wasn't there.

He told her about things she would once
have liked, and still did, according to him.
He asked her advice about the children
but didn't say if what she said was any help.

As I drifted off to sleep I wondered
if I could do that too – talk to him.
But when your own dear departed
is still living with his wife in Wembley
it's just not the same.

Before Dawn

PENELOPE SHUTTLE

I used to wake early, and weep.
Now I wake just as early,
calm as a cloud
in the moony sky outside.
Even thinking about unpaid bills
doesn't make me weep,
though I used to weep and weep.

4.30 a.m. No way of getting back
to sleep so I listen in
to the silence of a world dark and at rest.
I know other women
wider-awake than me.
I hear the silence beyond their weeping,
streetlamps outside their windows
won't blank out for hours and hours yet.

I used to wake early, etc …
Now I let my old friend Sleep
go his own sweet way,
listen to whoever is wide-awake in me,
running the flats of her hands

over the rough walls of the world,
looking for what?
A way in? A way out?
You tell me.

Care-charming Sleep

JOHN FLETCHER

Care-charming Sleep, thou easer of all woes,
Brother to Death, sweetly thyself dispose
On this afflicted prince; fall like a cloud
In gentle showers; give nothing that is loud
Or painful to his slumbers; easy, sweet,
And as a purling stream, thou son of Night,
Pass by his troubled senses; sing his pain,
Like hollow murmuring wind or silver rain;
Into this prince gently, oh gently slide,
And kiss him into slumbers like a bride.

Postscript

SEAMUS HEANEY

And some time make the time to drive out west
Into County Clare, along the Flaggy Shore,
In September or October, when the wind
And the light are working off each other
So that the ocean on one side is wild
With foam and glitter, and inland among stones
The surface of a slate-grey lake is lit
By the earthed lightning of a flock of swans,
Their feathers roughed and ruffling, white on white,
Their fully grown headstrong-looking heads
Tucked or cresting or busy underwater.
Useless to think you'll park and capture it
More thoroughly. You are neither here nor there,
A hurry through which known and strange things pass
As big soft buffetings come at the car sideways
And catch the heart off guard and blow it open.

Carpe diem

Seize the day! Live for the moment. Be truly present. Go with the flow.

These poems are for days when we feel anxious about the future, worry about money, our health or our loved ones. They help us to see hope and comfort in the smallest of things: flowers in a garden, washing fluttering on a line, horses running across a field – even reading a book of poetry. They are all about putting aside everyday worries and grabbing life with both hands.

What's Left

(for Peter Hennessy)

KERRY HARDIE

I used to wait for the flowers,
my pleasure reposed on them.
Now I like plants before they get to the blossom.
Leafy ones – foxgloves, comfrey, delphiniums –
fleshy tiers of strong leaves pushing up
into air grown daily lighter and more sheened
with bright dust like the eyeshadow
that tall young woman in the bookshop wears,
its shimmer and crumble on her white lids.

The washing sways on the line, the sparrows pull
at the heaps of drying weeds that I've left around.
Perhaps this is middle age. Untidy, unfinished,
knowing there'll never be time now to finish,
liking the plants – their strong lives –
not caring about flowers, sitting in weeds
to write things down, look at things,
watching the sway of shirts on the line,
the cloth filtering light.
I know more or less

how to live through my life now.
But I want to know how to live what's left
with my eyes open and my hands open;
I want to stand at the door in the rain
listening, sniffing, gaping.
Fearful and joyous,
like an idiot before God.

Pied Beauty

GERARD MANLEY HOPKINS

Glory be to God for dappled things –
    For skies of couple-colour as a brinded cow;
        For rose-moles all in stipple upon trout that swim;
Fresh-firecoal chestnut-falls; finches' wings;
    Landscape plotted and pieced – fold, fallow, and plough;
        And áll trádes, their gear and tackle and trim.
All things counter, original, spare, strange;
    Whatever is fickle, freckled (who knows how?)
        With swift, slow; sweet, sour; adazzle, dim;
He fathers-forth whose beauty is past change:
                    Praise him.

Lane

JONATHAN DAVIDSON

Cut into slabs of sandstone,
a drift of dead leaves lap
at its edges. To walk or cycle
down it is to enter the mind
of the pilgrim, the dark
striations are the claw marks
of good intentions and where
we are journeying will be
hot though the bosky shadows
make this lane cold. To rise
out of the sunken way, with
muscles aching from standing
on the pedals for leverage or
the heels' tendons stretched
and released in energetic
walking is to see the light
of days, of all our days, come
up into a plain horizon. And
suddenly we are out and on
top of the hill, with fields
and a nearby motorway

lying all around us and we
are unreasonably happy.

The world is too much with us

WILLIAM WORDSWORTH

The world is too much with us; late and soon,
Getting and spending, we lay waste our powers; –
Little we see in Nature that is ours;
We have given our hearts away, a sordid boon!
This Sea that bares her bosom to the moon;
The winds that will be howling at all hours,
And are up-gathered now like sleeping flowers;
For this, for everything, we are out of tune;
It moves us not. Great God! I'd rather be
A Pagan suckled in a creed outworn;
So might I, standing on this pleasant lea,
Have glimpses that would make me less forlorn;
Have sight of Proteus rising from the sea;
Or hear old Triton blow his wreathèd horn.

A Blessing

JAMES WRIGHT

Just off the highway to Rochester, Minnesota,
Twilight bounds softly forth on the grass.
And the eyes of those two Indian ponies
Darken with kindness.
They have come gladly out of the willows
To welcome my friend and me.
We step over the barbed wire into the pasture
Where they have been grazing all day, alone.
They ripple tensely, they can hardly contain their
    happiness
That we have come.
They bow shyly as wet swans. They love each other.
There is no loneliness like theirs.
At home once more,
They begin munching the young tufts of spring in the
    darkness.
I would like to hold the slenderer one in my arms,
For she has walked over to me
And nuzzled my left hand.
She is black and white,
Her mane falls wild on her forehead,
And the light breeze moves me to caress her long ear

That is delicate as the skin over a girl's wrist.
Suddenly I realize
That if I stepped out of my body I would break
Into blossom.

The Time Before Death
KABIR

Friend? hope for the Guest while you are alive.
Jump into experience while you are alive!
Think … and think … while you are alive.
What you call 'salvation' belongs to the time
    before death.

If you don't break your ropes while you're alive,
do you think ghosts will do it after?

The idea that the soul will rejoin with the ecstatic
just because the body is rotten –
that is all fantasy.
What is found now is found then.

If you find nothing now,
you will simply end up with an apartment in the
   City of Death.

If you make love with the divine now, in the next
life you will have the face of satisfied desire.

So plunge into the truth, find out who the Teacher is,
Believe in the Great Sound!

Kabir says this: When the Guest is being searched for,
it is the intensity of the longing for the Guest
that does all the work.

Look at me, and you will see a slave of that intensity.

To the Virgins, to Make Much of Time

ROBERT HERRICK

Gather ye rosebuds while ye may,
    Old Time is still a-flying;
And this same flower that smiles today
    Tomorrow will be dying.

The glorious lamp of heaven, the sun,
    The higher he's a-getting,
The sooner will his race be run,
    And nearer he's to setting.

That age is best which is the first,
    When youth and blood are warmer;
But being spent, the worse, and worst
    Times still succeed the former.

Then be not coy, but use your time,
    And while ye may, go marry;
For having lost but once your prime,
    You may forever tarry.

i thank You God

E. E. CUMMINGS

i thank You God for most this amazing
day: for the leaping greenly spirits of trees
and a blue true dream of sky; and for everything
which is natural which is infinite which is yes

(i who have died am alive again today,
and this is the sun's birthday; this is the birth
day of life and of love and wings: and of the gay
great happening illimitably earth)

how should tasting touching hearing seeing
breathing any – lifted from the no
of all nothing – human merely being
doubt unimaginable You?

(now the ears of my ears awake and
now the eyes of my eyes are opened)

Lines Composed a Few Miles Above Tintern Abbey [*extract*]

WILLIAM WORDSWORTH

And all its aching joys are now no more,
And all its dizzy raptures. Not for this
Faint I, nor mourn nor murmur; other gifts
Have followed, for such loss, I would believe,
Abundant recompence. For I have learned
To look on nature, not as in the hour
Of thoughtless youth, but hearing oftentimes
The still, sad music of humanity,
Nor harsh nor grating, though of ample power
To chasten and subdue. And I have felt
A presence that disturbs me with the joy
Of elevated thoughts; a sense sublime
Of something far more deeply interfused,
Whose dwelling is the light of setting suns,
And the round ocean, and the living air,
And the blue sky, and in the mind of man.

Now I become myself

As Jackie Kay says in her poem 'Somebody Else', many of us spend too long not being ourselves. These poems remind us of who we are, and that we should accept and love ourselves for who we are, warts and all. 'The Man on the Desert Island' tells us that it is only ourselves that we can hope to change.

Table

EDIP CANSEVER

A man filled with the gladness of living
Put his keys on the table,
Put flowers in a copper bowl there.
He put his eggs and milk on the table.
He put there the light that came in through the window,
Sounds of a bicycle, sound of a spinning wheel.
The softness of bread and weather he put there.
On the table the man put
Things that happened in his mind.
What he wanted to do in life,
He put that there.
Those he loved, those he didn't love,
The man put them on the table too.
Three times three make nine:
The man put nine on the table.
He was next to the window next to the sky;
He reached out and placed on the table endlessness.
So many days he had wanted to drink a beer!
He put on the table the pouring of that beer.
He placed there his sleep and his wakefulness;
His hunger and his fullness he placed there.

Now that's what I call a table!
It didn't complain at all about the load.
It wobbled once or twice, then stood firm.
The man kept piling things on.

Somebody Else
JACKIE KAY

If I was not myself, I would be somebody else.
But actually I am somebody else.
I have been somebody else all my life.

It's no laughing matter going about the place
all the time being somebody else:
people mistake you; you mistake yourself.

Now I become myself

MAY SARTON

Now I become myself. It's taken
Time, many years and places;
I have been dissolved and shaken,
Worn other people's faces,
Run madly, as if Time were there,
Terribly old, crying a warning,
'Hurry, you will be dead before –'
(What? Before you reach the morning?
Or the end of the poem is clear?
Or love safe in the walled city?)
Now to stand still, to be here,
Feel my own weight and density!
The black shadow on the paper
Is my hand; the shadow of a word
As thought shapes the shaper
Falls heavy on the page, is heard.
All fuses now, falls into place
From wish to action, word to silence,
My work, my love, my time, my face
Gathered into one intense
Gesture of growing like a plant.
As slowly as the ripening fruit

Fertile, detached, and always spent,
Falls but does not exhaust the root,
So all the poem is, can give,
Grows in me to become the song,
Made so and rooted by love.
Now there is time and Time is young.
O, in this single hour I live
All of myself and do not move.
I, the pursued, who madly ran,
Stand still, stand still, and stop the sun!

To be great, be whole

FERNANDO PESSOA

Translated from Romanian by Michael Impey and Brian Swann

To be great, be whole: don't exaggerate
Or leave out any part of you.
Be complete in each thing. Put all you are
Into the least of your acts.
So too in each lake, with it's lofty life,
The whole moon shines.

If you look for the truth outside yourself

TUNG-SHAN

If you look for the truth outside
      yourself,
it gets farther and farther away.
Today, walking alone,
I meet him everywhere I step.
He is the same as me,
yet, I am not him.
Only if you understand it in this way
will you merge with the way things are.

The Man on the Desert Island

GERDA MAYER

The man on the desert island
Has forgotten the ways of people,
His stories are all of himself.
Day in, day out of time,
He communes with himself and sends
Messages in green bottles:
Help me they say *I am*
Cast up and far from home.
Each day he goes to watch
The horizon for ships.
Nothing reaches his shore
Except corked green bottles.

No man is an island

JOHN DONNE

No man is an island entire of itself; every man
is a piece of the continent, a part of the main;
if a clod be washed away by the sea, Europe
is the less, as well as if a promontory were, as
well as any manner of thy friends or of thine
own were; any man's death diminishes me,
because I am involved in mankind.
And therefore never send to know for whom
the bell tolls; it tolls for thee.

I am!

JOHN CLARE

I am – yet what I am none cares or knows;
My friends forsake me like a memory lost:
I am the self-consumer of my woes –
They rise and vanish in oblivious host,
Like shadows in love's frenzied stifled throes
And yet I am, and live – like vapours tossed

Into the nothingness of scorn and noise,
Into the living sea of waking dreams,
Where there is neither sense of life or joys,
But the vast shipwreck of my life's esteems;
Even the dearest that I loved the best
Are strange – nay, rather, stranger than the rest.

I long for scenes where man hath never trod
A place where woman never smiled or wept
There to abide with my Creator, God,
And sleep as I in childhood sweetly slept,
Untroubling and untroubled where I lie
The grass below – above the vaulted sky.

You see, I desire a lot

RAINER MARIA RILKE

Translated by James Sheard

You see, I desire a lot.
Perhaps I desire it all:
Each eternal case of darkness
and each clambering-up to the playful light.
So many live and want nothing.
They crown themselves with smooth, small feelings
in the cool and empty courts. So
take pleasure in the faces
that serve and thirst for more.
Take pleasure in the ones who use you
Like an instrument. Because
you are not cold yet, and it is not too late
to plunge into your open depths – they wait,
silently, to unfold a life for you.

The Waking

THEODORE ROETHKE

I wake to sleep, and take my waking slow.
I feel my fate in what I cannot fear.
I learn by going where I have to go.

We think by feeling. What is there to know?
I hear my being dance from ear to ear.
I wake to sleep, and take my waking slow.

Of those so close beside me, which are you?
God bless the Ground! I shall walk softly there,
And learn by going where I have to go.

Light takes the Tree; but who can tell us how?
The lowly worm climbs up a winding stair;
I wake to sleep, and take my waking slow.

Great Nature has another thing to do
To you and me; so take the lively air,
And, lovely, learn by going where to go.

This shaking keeps me steady. I should know.
What falls away is always. And is near.
I wake to sleep, and take my waking slow.
I learn by going where I have to go.

Happy the man

JOHN DRYDEN

Happy the man, and happy he alone,
He who can call today his own:
He who, secure within, can say,
Tomorrow do thy worst, for I have lived today.
Be fair or foul or rain or shine
The joys I have possessed, in spite of fate, are mine.
Not Heaven itself upon the past has power,
But what has been, has been, and I have had my hour.

God Says Yes To Me

KAYLIN HAUGHT

I asked God if it was okay to be melodramatic
and she said yes
I asked her if it was okay to be short
and she said it sure is
I asked her if I could wear nail polish
or not wear nail polish
and she said honey
she calls me that sometimes
she said you can do just exactly
what you want to
Thanks God I said
And is it even okay if I don't paragraph
my letters
Sweetcakes God said
who knows where she picked that up
what I'm telling you is
Yes Yes Yes

Ordeal

NINA CASSIAN

Translated from the Portuguese by Richard Zenith

I promise to make you more alive than you've ever been.
For the first time you'll see your pores opening
like the gills of fish and you'll hear
the noise of blood in galleries
and feel light gliding on your corneas
like the dragging of a dress across the floor.
For the first time, you'll note gravity's prick
like a thorn in your heel,
and your shoulder blades will hurt from the imperative
    of wings.
I promise to make you so alive that
the fall of dust on furniture will deafen you,
and you'll feel your eyebrows like two wounds forming
and your memories will seem to begin
with the creation of the world.

Ecclesiastes, Chapter 3, Verses 1–8

KING JAMES BIBLE

To everything there is a season, and a time to every
purpose under the heaven:
a time to be born, and a time to die;
a time to plant, and a time to pluck up that which is
planted;
a time to kill, and a time to heal; a time to break down,
and a time to build up;
a time to weep, and a time to laugh; a time to mourn,
and a time to dance;
a time to cast away stones, and a time to gather stones
together;
a time to embrace, and a time to refrain from embracing;
a time to get, and a time to lose; a time to keep, and a
time to cast away;
a time to rend, and a time to sew; a time to keep silence,
and a time to speak;
a time to love, and a time to hate; a time of war, and a
time of peace.

LOVE

This chapter focuses on poems of love and marriage, of loves lost and looked for, of loving and letting go, love for children and for friends and that found in later life.

The poem I share perhaps more than any other is Derek Walcott's wise and difficult poem 'Love After Love.' The poem is tricky because it asks us to look in the mirror and be pleased with our reflection, rather than to seek out fulfilment only by being loved and through loving another.

First Love

JOHN CLARE

I ne'er was struck before that hour
 With love so sudden and so sweet,
Her face it bloomed like a sweet flower
 And stole my heart away complete.
My face turned pale as deadly pale,
 My legs refused to walk away,
And when she looked, what could I ail?
 My life and all seemed turned to clay.

And then my blood rushed to my face
 And took my eyesight quite away,
The trees and bushes round the place
 Seemed midnight at noonday.
I could not see a single thing,
 Words from my eyes did start—
They spoke as chords do from the string,
 And blood burnt round my heart.

Are flowers the winter's choice?
 Is love's bed always snow?
She seemed to hear my silent voice,

Not love's appeals to know.
I never saw so sweet a face
   As that I stood before.
My heart has left its dwelling-place
   And can return no more.

Green

D. H. LAWRENCE

The dawn was apple-green,
The sky was green wine held up in the sun,
The moon was a golden petal between.

She opened her eyes, and green
They shone, clear like flowers undone
For the first time, now for the first time seen.

A Birthday

CHRISTINA ROSSETTI

My heart is like a singing bird
 Whose nest is in a water'd shoot;
My heart is like an apple-tree
 Whose boughs are bent with thickset fruit;
My heart is like a rainbow shell
 That paddles in a halcyon sea;
My heart is gladder than all these
 Because my love is come to me.

Raise me a dais of silk and down;
 Hang it with vair and purple dyes;
Carve it in doves and pomegranates,
 And peacocks with a hundred eyes;
Work it in gold and silver grapes,
 In leaves and silver fleurs-de-lys;
Because the birthday of my life
 Is come, my love is come to me.

Love is ...

1 CORINTHIANS 13 (4–13)

Love is patient, love is kind. It does not envy, it does not boast, it is not proud. It does not dishonour others, it is not self-seeking, it is not easily angered, it keeps no record of wrongs. Love does not delight in evil but rejoices with the truth. It always protects, always trusts, always hopes, always perseveres.

Love never fails. But where there are prophecies, they will cease; where there are tongues, they will be stilled; where there is knowledge, it will pass away. For we know in part and we prophesy in part, but when completeness comes, what is in part disappears. When I was a child, I talked like a child, I thought like a child, I reasoned like a child. When I became a man, I put the ways of childhood behind me. For now we see only a reflection as in a mirror; then we shall see face to face. Now I know in part; then I shall know fully, even as I am fully known. And now these three remain: faith, hope and love. But the greatest of these is love.

The Sovereignty of Love

CHRISTINA ROSSETTI

If love is not worth loving, then life is not worth living,
    Nor aught is worth remembering but well forgot;
For store is not worth storing and gifts are not worth
        giving,
    If love is not;

    And idly cold is death-cold, and life-heat idly hot,
And vain is any offering and vainer our receiving,
    And vanity of vanities is all our lot.

Better than life's heaving heart is death's heart
        unheaving,
    Better than the opening leaves are the leaves that rot,
For there is nothing left worth achieving or retrieving,
    If love is not.

Friendship

ELIZABETH JENNINGS

Such love I cannot analyse;
It does not rest in lips or eyes,
Neither in kisses nor caress.
Partly, I know, it's gentleness

And understanding in one word
Or in brief letters. It's preserved
By trust and by respect and awe.
These are the words I'm feeling for.

Two people, yes, two lasting friends.
The giving comes, the taking ends
There is no measure for such things.
For this all Nature slows and sings.

Sonnet 116

WILLIAM SHAKESPEARE

Let me not to the marriage of true minds
Admit impediments. Love is not love
Which alters when it alteration finds,
Or bends with the remover to remove:
O no; it is an ever-fixed mark,
That looks on tempests, and is never shaken;
It is the star to every wandering bark,
Whose worth's unknown, although his height be taken.
Love's not Time's fool, though rosy lips and cheeks
Within his bending sickle's compass come;
Love alters not with his brief hours and weeks,
But bears it out even to the edge of doom.
    If this be error and upon me proved,
    I never writ, nor no man ever loved.

You were the one lost

RAINER MARIA RILKE

Translated by James Sheard

You were the one
lost from the start, love, the one who never came,
and I was never to know which songs would please you.
So I will no longer try to know you, as these moments
pile in on me like waves. All the great imaginings
in me, and in the distant, deep-felt landscape –
the cities and towers and bridges, and the un-
guessed-at turns in the untaken paths,
and the Godlike force that once pulsed in my country –
all these rise up in me and speak only of you
and of how you will elude me forever.

Ah, you are the gardens, yes,
the ones I looked at with such
hope. The open window
of a country house, you stepping past
and pausing, and almost coming to me.
There are narrow streets
down which you have just passed, and passed on,
and sometimes shop mirrors which shiver

as if you were seen in them – these shock me back
to my image of you. And who knows, who knows
if the same bird does not sing out
and through us both, whether
yesterday, or separately, or in the evening?

The Lover in Winter Plaineth for the Spring

ANONYMOUS

O WESTERN wind, when wilt thou blow
    That the small rain down can rain?
Christ, that my love were in my arms
    And I in my bed again!

Outgrown

PENELOPE SHUTTLE

It is both sad and a relief to fold so carefully
her outgrown clothes and line up the little worn shoes
of childhood, so prudent, scuffed and particular.
It is both happy and horrible to send them galloping
back tappity-tap along the mist chill path into the past.

It is both a freedom and a prison, to be outgrown
by her as she towers over me as thin as a sequin
in her doc martens and her pretty skirt
because just as I work out how to be a mother
she stops being a child.

One Art

ELIZABETH BISHOP

The art of losing isn't hard to master;
so many things seem filled with the intent
to be lost that their loss is no disaster.

Lose something every day. Accept the fluster
of lost door keys, the hour badly spent.
The art of losing isn't hard to master.

Then practice losing farther, losing faster:
places, and names, and where it was you meant
to travel. None of these will bring disaster.

I lost my mother's watch. And look! my last, or
next-to-last, of three loved houses went.
The art of losing isn't hard to master.

I lost two cities, lovely ones. And, vaster,
some realms I owned, two rivers, a continent.
I miss them, but it wasn't a disaster.

– Even losing you (the joking voice, a gesture
I love) I shan't have lied. It's evident
the art of losing's not too hard to master
though it may look like (*Write* it!) a disaster.

Donal Og

GAELIC EIGHTH-CENTURY IRISH BALLAD

Translated by Lady Augusta Gregory

It is late last night the dog was speaking of you;
the snipe was speaking of you in her deep marsh.
It is you are the lonely bird through the woods;
and that you may be without a mate until you find me.

You promised me, and you said a lie to me,
that you would be before me where the sheep are
    flocked;
I gave a whistle and three hundred cries to you,
and I found nothing there but a bleating lamb.

You promised me a thing that was hard for you,
a ship of gold under a silver mast;
twelve towns with a market in all of them,
and a fine white court by the side of the sea.

You promised me a thing that is not possible,
that you would give me gloves of the skin of a fish;
that you would give me shoes of the skin of a bird;
and a suit of the dearest silk in Ireland.

When I go by myself to the Well of Loneliness,
I sit down and I go through my trouble;
when I see the world and do not see my boy,
he that has an amber shade in his hair.

It was on that Sunday I gave my love to you;
the Sunday that is last before Easter Sunday
and myself on my knees reading the Passion;
and my two eyes giving love to you for ever.

My mother has said to me not to be talking with you
    today,
or tomorrow, or on the Sunday;

it was a bad time she took for telling me that;
it was shutting the door after the house was robbed.

My heart is as black as the blackness of the sloe,
or as the black coal that is on the smith's forge;
or as the sole of a shoe left in white halls;
it was you put that darkness over my life.

You have taken the east from me, you have taken the
    west from me;
you have taken what is before me and what is behind me;
you have taken the moon, you have taken the sun from me;
and my fear is great that you have taken God from me!

Piano

D. H. LAWRENCE

Softly, in the dusk, a woman is singing to me;
Taking me back down the vista of years, till I see
A child sitting under the piano, in the boom of the
    tingling strings
And pressing the small, poised feet of a mother who
    smiles as she sings.

In spite of myself, the insidious mastery of song
Betrays me back, till the heart of me weeps to belong
To the old Sunday evenings at home, with winter outside
And hymns in the cosy parlour, the tinkling piano our
    guide.

So now it is vain for the singer to burst into clamour
With the great black piano appassionato. The glamour
Of childish days is upon me, my manhood is cast
Down in the flood of remembrance, I weep like a child
    for the past.

Love After Love

DEREK WALCOTT

The time will come
when, with elation
you will greet yourself arriving
at your own door, in your own mirror
and each will smile at the other's welcome,

and say, sit here. Eat.
You will love again the stranger who was your self.
Give wine. Give bread. Give back your heart
to itself, to the stranger who has loved you

all your life, whom you ignored
for another, who knows you by heart.
Take down the love letters from the bookshelf,

the photographs, the desperate notes,
peel your own image from the mirror.
Sit. Feast on your life.

Apron Strings

STEVE HARRISON

I could never strain the spuds
with just the lid, like mum did;
that deft hold at the right angle
to do the job.

I could never make batter
without spooning flour or measuring milk,
so in answer to my long distance *how much?*
Enough, would suffice as her telephoned advice.

Now my hands, flaking with flour
in her familiar cracked mixing bowl,
yoke yellow on the outside,
fried egg white in the middle.

Passed down fingers begin to ache
and twist to similar degrees,
as the mind begins to loose its apron strings.

The smoke alarm that detects hot forgotten fat,
has let the molten lard reach the right explosive mix,

hot enough for batter.
This time, it would do the job for mum.

Late

JAMES SHEARD

You could be my garden, for think how gardens
can be our last and best love, our late love,
brought up and out of our earth and made to bloom.

Think how we bring to them our lifetime of care,
Our longing for a place to lie in and call our own.
That is why I brought you here in late Summer,

to watch you walk up through the blown grasses
and their feathery tops moving gently around you.
You came to me, slowly, down the long shade

of the laburnum arch, as if approaching shyly
from the long years of my early and middle life -
dappled and distant, but coming on, coming on.

Kissing

FLEUR ADCOCK

The young are walking on the riverbank
arms around each other's waist and shoulders,
pretending to be looking at the waterlilies
and what might be a nest of some kind, over
there, which two who are clamped together
mouth to mouth have forgotten about.
The others, making courteous detours
around them, talk, stop talking, kiss.
They can see no one older than themselves.
It's their river. They've got all day.

Seeing's not everything. At this very
moment the middle-aged are kissing
in the backs of taxis, on the way
to airports and stations. Their mouths and tongues
are soft and powerful and as moist as ever.
Their hands are not inside each other's clothes
(because of the driver) but locked so tightly
together that it hurts: it may leave marks
on their not of course youthful skin, which they won't
notice. They too may have futures.

A Short Piece of Choral Music

JONATHAN DAVIDSON

It's an evening in late March and in the kitchen
I'm listening to a short piece of choral music,
when my son comes in to fetch himself a bowl
of breakfast cereal which, he tells me, helps
with his revision. And another thing, he goes on,
I shouldn't worry about him because he's going
to be fine: exams, work, life, everything, is going
to be fine. That's a relief, I say to myself, thanks,
now I can listen to this music, which turns out
to be just some fancy noise, nothing
compared with a boy's cheerfulness.

Later Love

LIZ LEFROY

This later love is better, worse,
knows all, forgives, but not all,
is filled with the contradictions

of terror and lust, desiring
both distance, and sudden intimacy.
It shadows itself, is itself shadowed

by recollections not its own.
It is the palate of the wise,
and has forgotten what this tasted like.

This love is so slender, it mends itself
and everything that it will break.
I know it. It will. It will.

Huge Blue

(For Jack)

PIPPA LITTLE

You were three when we moved north,
near the sea. That first time
you took one look, twisted off your clothes
till, bare as the day you were born,

you made off: I had to sprint,
scoop you up just as you threw the whole of you
into its huge blue – or you might be swimming still,
half way to Murmansk, that port you always dreamed of
   seeing:

I once flew, about your age:
strong arms held me hard,
hauled me down so my salted eyelashes
stuck together, sucked blue dark:

I didn't know how to remember
until you opened your arms that day,
sure that the world would hold you
and it did: grown now, and half a world away,

I hope your huge blue
is beautiful with stars
as you leap, eyes wide open,
no ghost of me on your back.

Walking Away

(For Sean)

C. DAY LEWIS

It is eighteen years ago, almost to the day –
A sunny day with the leaves just turning,
The touch-lines new-ruled – since I watched you play
Your first game of football, then, like a satellite
Wrenched from its orbit, go drifting away

Behind a scatter of boys. I can see
You walking away from me towards the school
with the pathos of a half-fledged thing set free
Into a wilderness, the gait of one
Who finds no path where the path should be.

That hesitant figure, eddying away
Like a winged seed loosened from its parent stem,
Has something I never quite grasp to convey
About nature's give-and-take – the small, the scorching
Ordeals which fire one's irresolute clay.

I had worse partings, but none that so
Gnaws at my mind still. Perhaps it is roughly
Saying what God alone could perfectly show –
How selfhood begins with a walking away,
And love proved in the letting go.

Love and Friendship

EMILY BRONTË

Love is like the wild rose-briar,
Friendship like the holly-tree –
The holly is dark when the rose-briar blooms
But which will bloom most constantly?

The wild rose-briar is sweet in spring,
Its summer blossoms scent the air;
Yet wait till winter comes again
And who will call the wild-briar fair?

Then scorn the silly rose-wreath now
And deck thee with the holly's sheen,
That when December blights thy brow
He still may leave thy garland green.

The Confirmation

EDWIN MUIR

Yes, yours, my love, is the right human face,
I in my mind had waited for this long,
Seeing the false and searching for the true,
Then found you as a traveller finds a place
Of welcome suddenly amid the wrong
Valleys and rocks and twisting roads. But you,
What shall I call you? A fountain in a waste,
A well of water in a country dry,
Or anything that's honest and good, an eye
That makes the whole world bright. Your open heart,
Simple with giving, gives the primal deed,
The first good world, the blossom, the blowing seed,
The hearth, the steadfast land, the wandering sea.
Not beautiful or rare in every part.
But like yourself, as they were meant to be.

GETTING OLDER

Elaine Feinstein's poem 'Getting Older' is effective medicine against the feeling that getting older is a miserable experience, and tells us to enjoy the unexpected fruits of this final stage in our lives, rather than fear it.

Getting Older

ELAINE FEINSTEIN

The first surprise: I like it.
Whatever happens now, some things
that used to terrify have not:

I didn't die young, for instance. Or lose
my only love. My three children
never had to run away from anyone.

Don't tell me this gratitude is complacent.
We all approach the edge of the same blackness
which for me is silent.

Knowing as much sharpens
my delight in January freesia,
hot coffee, winter sunlight. So we say

as we lie close on some gentle occasion:
every day won from such
darkness is a celebration.

Elegy for a Walnut Tree

W. S. MERWIN

Old friend now there is no one alive
who remembers when you were young
it was high summer when I first saw you
in the blaze of day most of my life ago
with the dry grass whispering in your shade
and already you had lived through wars
and echoes of wars around your silence
through days of parting and seasons of absence
with the house emptying as the years went their way
until it was home to bats and swallows
and still when spring climbed toward summer
you opened once more the curled sleeping fingers
of newborn leaves as though nothing had happened
you and the seasons spoke the same language
and all these years I have looked through your limbs
to the river below and the roofs and the night
and you were the way I saw the world

When you are old

WILLIAM BUTLER YEATS

When you are old and grey and full of sleep,
And nodding by the fire, take down this book,
And slowly read, and dream of the soft look
Your eyes had once, and of their shadows deep;

How many loved your moments of glad grace,
And loved your beauty with love false or true,
But one man loved the pilgrim soul in you,
And loved the sorrows of your changing face;

And bending down beside the glowing bars,
Murmur, a little sadly, how Love fled
And paced upon the mountains overhead
And hid his face amid a crowd of stars.

The Way Through the Woods

RUDYARD KIPLING

They shut the road through the woods
Seventy years ago.
Weather and rain have undone it again,
And now you would never know
There was once a road through the woods
Before they planted the trees.
It is underneath the coppice and heath,
And the thin anemones.
Only the keeper sees
That, where the ring-dove broods,
And the badgers roll at ease,
There was once a road through the woods.

Yet, if you enter the woods
Of a summer evening late,
When the night-air cools on the trout-ringed pools
Where the otter whistles his mate,
(They fear not men in the woods,
Because they see so few.)
You will hear the beat of a horse's feet,
And the swish of a skirt in the dew,

Steadily cantering through
The misty solitudes,
As though they perfectly knew
The old lost road through the woods.
But there is no road through the woods.

Rondeau

LEIGH HUNT

Jenny kissed me when we met,
   Jumping from the chair she sat in;
Time, you thief, who love to get
   Sweets into your list, put that in:
Say I'm weary, say I'm sad,
   Say that health and wealth have missed me,
Say I'm growing old, but add,
   Jenny kissed me.

A Shropshire Lad [*extract*]

A. E. HOUSMAN

XXXIX

'Tis time, I think, by Wenlock town
　　The golden broom should blow;
The hawthorn sprinkled up and down
　　Should charge the land with snow.

Spring will not wait the loiterer's time
　　Who keeps so long away;
So others wear the broom and climb
　　The hedgerows heaped with may.

Oh tarnish late on Wenlock Edge,
　　Gold that I never see;
Lie long, high snowdrifts in the hedge
　　That will not shower on me.

XL

Into my heart an air that kills
　　From yon far country blows:
What are those blue remembered hills,
　　What spires, what farms are those?

That is the land of lost content,
    I see it shining plain,
The happy highways where I went
    And cannot come again.

Heredity

THOMAS HARDY

I am the family face;
Flesh perishes, I live on,
Projecting trait and trace
Through time to times anon,
And leaping from place to place
Over oblivion.

The years-heired feature that can
In curve and voice and eye
Despise the human span
Of durance – that is I;
The eternal thing in man,
That heeds no call to die.

John Anderson my jo, John

ROBERT BURNS

John Anderson my jo, John,
    When we were first acquent,
Your locks were like the raven,
    Your bonie brow was brent;
But now your brow is beld, John,
    Your locks are like the snaw,
but blessings on your frosty pow,
    John Anderson, my jo!

John Anderson my jo, John,
    We clamb the hill thegither,
And monie a cantie day, John,
    We've had wi' ane anither;
Now we maun totter down, John,
    And hand in hand we'll go,
And sleep thegither at the foot,
    John Anderson, my jo!

The Seed Shop

MURIEL STUART

Here in a quiet and dusty room they lie,
Faded as crumbled stone or shifting sand,
Forlorn as ashes, shrivelled, scentless, dry –
Meadows and gardens running through my hand.

Dead that shall quicken at the call of Spring,
Sleepers to stir beneath June's magic kiss,
Though birds pass over, unremembering,
And no bee seek here roses that were his.

In this brown husk a dale of hawthorn dreams;
A cedar in this narrow cell is thrust
That will drink deeply of a century's streams;
These lilies shall make summer on my dust.

Here in their safe and simple house of death,
Sealed in their shells, a million roses leap;
Here I can blow a garden with my breath,
And in my hand a forest lies asleep.

Time flies

FOUND ON AN ENGLISH SUNDIAL

Time flies, Suns rise
And shadows fall.
Let time go by.
Love is forever over all.

BE ALIVE EVERY MINUTE OF YOUR LIFE

This section concerns illness and how to deal with it. There is sure to be something that will touch on a personal experience, from Char March's affectionate portrait of a mother after a mastectomy, Myra Schneider's poem 'The Red Dress' – a personal account of coming to terms with her own changed body – and 'Flight', which speaks of recovery from mental ill health, to poems that comfort and reassure even when they recognize moments of fear. And as Schneider reminds us in her poem, 'be alive every minute of your life'.

The Red Dress

MYRA SCHNEIDER

My first reaction is: I want it,
can't wait to squeeze into
a scarlet sheath that promises
breasts round as russet apples,
a waist pinched to a pencil,
hips that know the whole dictionary
of swaying, can't wait
to saunter down an August street
with every eye upon me.

But the moment I'm zipped in
I can't breathe and the fabric
hugging my stomach without mercy
pronounces me a frump.
Besides, in the internet café,
where you can phone Tangiers
or Thailand for almost nothing
fourteen pairs of eyes
are absorbed by screens.

No one whistles when I smile
at boxes of tired mangoes
and seedy broccoli heads
outside the Greek superstore.

By now I'm in a fever to undo
the garment and pull it off.
And for all its flaws, for all
that it only boasts one breast,
I'm overjoyed to re-possess
my body. I remember I hate
holding in and shutting away.
What I want is a dress easy
as a plump plum oozing
juice, as a warm afternoon
in late October creeping
its ambers and cinnamons into
leaves, a dress that reassures
there's no need to pretend,
a dress that's as capacious
as generosity, a dress that willingly
unbuttons and whispers in the ear:
be alive every minute of your life.

Tracks

TOMAS TRANSTRÖMER

Translated from the Swedish by Robin Fulton

2 am: moonlight. The train has stopped
out in the middle of the plain. Far away, points of light in
   a town,
flickering coldly at the horizon.

As when a man has gone into a dream so deep
he'll never remember having been there
when he comes back to his room.

As when someone has gone into an illness so deep
everything his days were becomes a few flickering points,
   a swarm,
cold and tiny at the horizon.

The train is standing quite still.
2 am: bright moonlight, few stars.

Shoe Trap

WENDY PRATT

In the dark I grope across the bedroom
floor, feel for the shape of the wall, the door
and half trip, half step over your work shoes.
Shoe trap. Your favourite trick, four
shoes, haphazardly strewn,
your habit. *My* habit is the stumble, the meeting
of floor and face, the standard bruise
to the knee. Your shoe trap has held me captive
for thirteen years, swearing in the dark on my way
to the bathroom. Your habits and mine; a dance,
a meeting of selves over and over. The day
after my sister loses her husband to cancer,
I trip on your shoes in the dark, holding their scrubby,
battered shape, I've never felt so blessed or lucky.

Drawing Him at Fifty

ROZ GODDARD

She takes him into the garden
where the leaves of a beech are lit
with the last of the January sun –
instructs him to lean on a stone bench
and look at what he finds interesting.
She drew him at Twenty, when his broad shoulders held
    up the sky
At Thirty, his foot steady on a spade
At Forty, laughing at his own awful joke.
And now at Fifty – as the disease gradually erases him.
He's looking at her and smiling – she is what interests
    him still.
She would like to go back to the beginning, start again
    and again
reach into the future and stare out at the horizon.
The Archbishop speaks of heroes who live in long
    marriages
and the sweet struggle of love.
So she draws him with her icy eye, her broken heart –
every charcoal line, every smudge of him.

When I have fears that I may cease to be

JOHN KEATS

When I have fears that I may cease to be
   Before my pen has gleaned my teeming brain,
Before high-pilèd books, in charactery,
   Hold like rich garners the full ripened grain;
When I behold, upon the night's starred face,
   Huge cloudy symbols of a high romance,
And think that I may never live to trace
   Their shadows with the magic hand of chance;
And when I feel, fair creature of an hour,
   That I shall never look upon thee more,
Never have relish in the faery power
   Of unreflecting love—then on the shore
Of the wide world I stand alone, and think
Till love and fame to nothingness do sink.

Flight

SARAH WARDLE

The mother blackbird I've been feeding
has flown in the open door of the kitchen,
where she flutters against the stuck window,
like a butterfly, finding no way through.

A startled eye stares. In the flap of a wing
it all comes back: my heart beating
so fast I thought it would explode,
my mind and body in overload,

running the corridors, fleeing nurses,
who seemed stranger than another species
then trapped in a room with nowhere to go,
how I was cornered at a safety window,

which opened only far enough for air,
how I didn't know there was no cause for fear,
how they outnumbered me, fastened their grip,
laid me down and injected me, like rape.

I cup the bird gently in my hands, like water,
carry her out, as if a Section order
has been lifted, give her to the air,
then watch her spread her wings and soar.

Another box of nipples arrived today

CHAR MARCH

The hospital computer's gone mad
– that's the third box this week.
You stick them on the fridge door,
the phone, the handle of the kettle.
And we laugh. Then you are sick again.

This evening you sit in your usual chair
in the bloat of chemo, your breath really
bothering you. And me, if truth be told.
You are darning pullovers neither of us
ever wear – and even Oxfam won't take.

What if I could give you a new pair?
That will always pass the pencil test, even
at 90; with velvet-dark areolae
and pert tips that jut cheekily, but
don't show through your tennis dress.

You are muttering about camels
and licking the thread for the nth time;
specs half-way down – in your usual chair.
I don't see hacked-at womanhood,
that you've sobbed salt-herring barrels for.

I see you. Darning your way to normality.

My own heart

GERARD MANLEY HOPKINS

My own heart let me more have pity on; let
Me live to my sad self hereafter kind,
Charitable; not live this tormented mind
With this tormented mind tormenting yet.
I cast for comfort I can no more get
By groping round my comfortless, than blind
Eyes in their dark can day or thirst can find
Thirst's all-in-all in all a world of wet.

Soul, self; come, poor Jackself, I do advise
You, jaded, let be; call off thoughts awhile
Elsewhere; leave comfort root-room; let joy size
At God knows when to God knows what; whose smile
's not wrung, see you; unforeseen times rather – as skies
Betweenpie mountains – lights a lovely mile.

Proverb

MOLLY HOLDEN

I am determined not to miss
one nuance of the light
on spire and tree
this bright September evening.
So I sit and stare,
the washing-up undone, the cat
unfed, watching the sunset penetrate
pinnacle and bell-tower louvre
of the church, fine-fingered leaves
and conker cases of the golden tree.
The oak's oil-brown, the ash
still green. The grass I cannot see
must strike up damp but rosy-crowned
with the last sunlight
slanting down the hill. I cannot
go out into that evening but my spies,
memory and imagination,
report back faithfully. I recall
the Chinese proverb about selling
half of one's last loaf to buy
flowers for the soul but I wonder,

if I had the choice now, whether
I'd have longer years of ordinary life
or this half-life and the tingle
of senses extra-sharp to beauty
as now sit contemplating dusk.

Of You

NORMAN MACCAIG

When the little devil, panic,
begins to grin and jump about
in my heart, in my brain, in my muscles,
I am shown the path I had lost
in the mountainy mist.

I'm writing of you.

When the pain that will kill me
is about to be unbearable,
a cool hand

puts a tablet on my tongue and the pain
dwindles away and vanishes.

I'm writing of you.

There are fires to be suffered,
the blaze of cruelty, the smoulder
of inextinguishable longing, even
the gentle candleflame of peace
that burns too.

I suffer them. I survive.

I'm writing of you.

The Weighing

JANE HIRSHFIELD

The heart's reasons
seen clearly,
even the hardest
will carry
its whip-marks and sadness
and must be forgiven.

As the drought-starved
eland forgives
the drought-starved lion
who finally takes her,
enters willingly then
the life she cannot refuse,
and is lion, is fed,
and does not remember the other.

So few grains of happiness
measured against all the dark
and still the scales balance.

The world asks of us
only the strength we have and we give it.
Then it asks more, and we give it.

The Song of a Man Who Has Come Through

D. H. LAWRENCE

Not I, not I, but the wind that blows through me!
A fine wind is blowing the new direction of Time.
If only I let it bear me, carry me, if only it carry me!
If only I am sensitive, subtle, oh, delicate, a winged gift!
If only, most lovely of all, I yield myself and am borrowed
By the fine, fine wind that takes its course through the
    chaos of the world
Like a fine, and exquisite chisel, a wedge-blade inserted;
If only I am keen and hard like the sheer tip of a wedge
Driven by invisible blows
The rock will split, we shall come at the wonder, we shall
    find the Hesperides

Oh, for the wonder that bubbles into my soul,
I would be a good fountain, a good well-head,
Would blur no whisper, spoil no expression.

What is the knocking?
What is the knocking at the door in the night?
It's somebody wants to do us harm.

No, no, it is the three strange angels.
Admit them, admit them.

Long Life

ELAINE FEINSTEIN

Late Summer. Sunshine. The eucalyptus tree.
   It is a fortune beyond any deserving
to be still *here*, with no more than everyday worries,
   placidly arranging lines of poetry.

I consider a stick of cinammon
   bound in raffia, finches

in the grass, and a stubby bush
    which this year mothered a lemon.

These days I speak less of death
    than the mysteries of survival. I am
no longer lonely, not yet frail, and
    after surgery, recognize each breath

as a miracle. My generation may not be
    nimble but, forgive us,
we'd like to hold on, stubbornly
    content – even while ageing.

Sonnet 318. On His Blindness

JOHN MILTON

WHEN I consider how my light is spent
　　E're half my days, in this dark world and wide,
　　And that one Talent which is death to hide,
　　Lodg'd with me useless, though my Soul more bent
To serve therewith my Maker, and present
　　My true account, least he returning chide,
　　Doth God exact day-labour, light deny'd,
　　I fondly ask; But patience to prevent
That murmur, soon replies, God doth not need
　　Either man's work or his own gifts, who best
　　Bear his milde yoak, they serve him best, his State
Is Kingly. Thousands at his bidding speed
　　And post o're Land and Ocean without rest:
　　They also serve who only stand and waite.

TALKING TO GRIEF

Most of us, at some point, have been through times of terrible pain and loss. These poems bring the kind of comfort that comes from sitting alongside someone who understands, who has been there before you and has come through it. The verses speak intimately and with kindness, and ask us to not be afraid of pain or the passing of someone much loved, but to allow ourselves to feel it, and ultimately, to let the loved one go.

Psalm 102 (1–7)

THE BIBLE (NEW INTERNATIONAL VERSION)

Hear my prayer, O Lord;
   let my cry for help come to you.
Do not hide your face from me
   when I am in distress.
Turn your ear to me;
   when I call, answer me quickly.

For my days vanish like smoke;
   my bones burn like glowing embers.
My heart is blighted and withered like grass;
   I forget to eat my food.
In my distress I groan aloud
   and am reduced to skin and bones.
I am like a desert owl,
   like an owl among the ruins.
I lie awake; I have become
   like a bird alone on a roof.

Up-Hill

CHRISTINA ROSSETTI

Does the road wind up-hill all the way?
    Yes, to the very end.
Will the day's journey take the whole long day?
    From morn to night, my friend.

But is there for the night a resting-place?
    A roof for when the slow dark hours begin.
May not the darkness hide it from my face?
    You cannot miss that inn.

Shall I meet other wayfarers at night?
    Those who have gone before.
Then must I knock, or call when just in sight?
    They will not keep you standing at that door.

Shall I find comfort, travel-sore and weak?
    Of labour you shall find the sum.
Will there be beds for me and all who seek?
    Yea, beds for all who come.

The Garden of Proserpine [*extract*]

A. C. SWINBURNE

We are not sure of sorrow,
   And joy was never sure;
To-day will die tomorrow;
   Time stoops to no man's lure;
And love grown faint and fretful,
With lips but half regretful
Sighs, and with eyes forgetful
   Weeps that no loves endure.

From too much love of living,
   From hope and fear set free,
We thank with brief thanksgiving
   Whatever gods may be
That no life lives for ever,
That dead men rise up never;
That even the weariest river
   Winds somewhere safe to sea.

No Taxis Available

BRIAN PATTEN

It is absurd not knowing where to go.

You wear the streets like an overcoat.
Certain houses are friends, certain houses
Can no longer be visited.
Old love affairs lurk in doorways, behind windows
Women grow older. Neglection blossoms.

You have turned down numerous invitations,
Left the telephones unanswered, said 'No'
To the few that needed you.
Stranded on an island of your own invention
You have thrown out messages, longings.

How useless it is knowing that where you want to go
Is nowhere concrete.
The trains will not take you there,
The red buses glide past without stopping,

No taxis are available.

East Coker [*extract*]

T. S. ELIOT

I said to my soul, be still, and let the dark come upon you
Which shall be the darkness of God. As, in a theatre,
The lights are extinguished, for the scene to be changed
With a hollow rumble of wings, with a movement of
    darkness on darkness,
And we know that the hills and the trees, the distant
    panorama
And the bold imposing facade are all being rolled away –
Or as, when an underground train, in the tube, stops too
    long between stations
And the conversation rises and slowly fades into silence
And you see behind every face the mental emptiness
    deepen
Leaving only the growing terror of nothing to think
    about;
Or when, under ether, the mind is conscious but
    conscious of nothing –
I said to my soul, be still, and wait without hope
For hope would be hope for the wrong thing; wait
    without love,

For love would be love of the wrong thing; there is yet
    faith
But the faith and the love and the hope are all in the
    waiting.
Wait without thought, for you are not ready for thought:
So the darkness shall be the light, and the stillness
    the dancing.

To Know the Dark

WENDELL BERRY

To go in the dark with a light is to know the light.
To know the dark, go dark. Go without sight,
and find that the dark, too, blooms and sings
and is traveled by dark feet and dark wings.

The Old Stoic

EMILY BRONTË

Riches I hold in light esteem,
    And Love I laugh to scorn;
And lust of fame was but a dream,
    That vanished with the morn:

And if I pray, the only prayer
    That moves my lips for me
Is, 'Leave the heart that now I bear,
    And give me liberty!'

Yes, as my swift days near their goal:
    'Tis all that I implore;
In life and death a chainless soul,
    With courage to endure.

Burlap Sack

JANE HIRSHFIELD

A person is full of sorrow
The way a burlap sack is full of stones or sand.
We say, 'Hand me the sack,'
But we get the weight.
Heavier if left out in the rain.
To think that the stones or sand are the self is an error.
To think that grief is the self is an error.
Self carries grief as a pack mule carries the side bags,
Being careful between the trees to leave extra room.
The self is not the load of ropes and nails and axes.
The self is not the miner nor builder nor driver.
What would it be to take the bride
And leave behind the heavy dowry?
To let the thin-ribbed mule browse in tall grasses,
Its long ears waggling like the tails of two happy dogs?

Song

CHRISTINA ROSSETTI

When I am dead, my dearest,
    Sing no sad songs for me;
Plant thou no roses at my head,
    Nor shady cypress tree:
Be the green grass above me
    With showers and dewdrops wet;
And if thou wilt, remember,
    And if thou wilt, forget.

I shall not see the shadows,
    I shall not feel the rain;
I shall not hear the nightingale
    Sing on, as if in pain:
And dreaming through the twilight
    That doth not rise nor set,
Haply I may remember,
    And haply may forget.

Talking to Grief

DENISE LEVERTOV

Ah, Grief, I should not treat you
like a homeless dog
who comes to the back door
for a crust, for a meatless bone.
I should trust you.

I should coax you
into the house and give you
your own corner,
a worn mat to lie on,
your own water dish.

You think I don't know you've been living
under my porch.
You long for your real place to be readied
before winter comes. You need
your name,
your collar and tag. You need
the right to warn off intruders,

to consider
my house your own
and me your person
and yourself
my own dog.

Everything Is Going to Be All Right

DEREK MAHON

How should I not be glad to contemplate
the clouds clearing beyond the dormer window
and a high tide reflected on the ceiling?
There will be dying, there will be dying,
but there is no need to go into that.
The poems flow from the hand unbidden
and the hidden source is the watchful heart.
The sun rises in spite of everything
and the far cities are beautiful and bright.
I lie here in a riot of sunlight
watching the day break and the clouds flying.
Everything is going to be all right.

After great pain, a formal feeling comes

EMILY DICKINSON

After great pain, a formal feeling comes –
The Nerves sit ceremonious, like Tombs –
The stiff Heart questions 'was it He, that bore',
And 'Yesterday, or Centuries before'?

The Feet, mechanical, go round –
A Wooden way
Of Ground, or Air, or Ought –
Regardless grown,
A Quartz contentment, like a stone –

This is the Hour of Lead –
Remembered, if outlived,
As Freezing persons, recollect the Snow –
First – Chill – then Stupor – then the letting go –

The Unprofessionals

U. A. FANTHORPE

When the worst thing happens,
That uproots the future,
That you must live for every hour of your future,

They come,
Unorganized, inarticulate, unprofessional;

They come sheepishly, sit with you, holding hands,
From tea to tea, from Anadin to Valium,
Sleeping on put-you-ups, answering the phone,
Coming in shifts, spontaneously,

Talking sometimes,
About wallflowers, and fishing, and why
Dealing with Kleenex and kettles,
Doing the washing up and the shopping,

Like civilians in a shelter, under bombardment,
Holding hands and sitting it out
Through the immortality of all the seconds,
Until the blunting of time.

Native American Prayer

ANONYMOUS

When I am dead
Cry for me a little
Think of me sometimes
But not too much

Think of me now and again
As I was in life
At some moments it's pleasant to recall
But not for long

Leave me in peace
And I shall leave you in peace
And while you live
Let your thoughts be with the living

Remember

CHRISTINA ROSSETTI

Remember me when I am gone away,
   Gone far away into the silent land;
   When you can no more hold me by the hand,
Nor I half turn to go yet turning stay.
Remember me when no more day by day
   You tell me of our future that you plann'd:
   Only remember me; you understand
It will be late to counsel then or pray.
Yet if you should forget me for a while
   And afterwards remember, do not grieve:
   For if the darkness and corruption leave
   A vestige of the thoughts that once I had,
Better by far you should forget and smile
   Than that you should remember and be sad.

Do not stand at my grave and weep

MARY ELIZABETH FRYE

Do not stand at my grave and weep
I am not there. I do not sleep.
I am a thousand winds that blow.
I am the diamond glints on snow.
I am the sunlight on ripened grain.
I am the gentle autumn rain.
When you awaken in the morning's hush
I am the swift uplifting rush
Of quiet birds in circled flight.
I am the soft stars that shine at night.
Do not stand at my grave and cry;
I am not there. I did not die.

The Soldier

RUPERT BROOKE

If I should die, think only this of me:
    That there's some corner of a foreign field
That is forever England. There shall be
    In that rich earth a richer dust concealed;
A dust whom England bore, shaped, made aware,
    Gave, once, her flowers to love, her ways to roam,
A body of England's, breathing English air,
    Washed by the rivers, blest by the suns of home.

And think, this heart, all evil shed away,
    A pulse in the eternal mind, no less
        Gives somewhere back the thoughts by England given;
Her sights and sounds; dreams happy as her day;
    And laughter, learnt of friends; and gentleness,
        In hearts at peace, under an English heaven.

The Embrace

MARK DOTY

You weren't well or really ill yet either;
just a little tired, your handsomeness
tinged by grief or anticipation, which brought
to your face a thoughtful, deepening grace.

I didn't for a moment doubt you were dead.
I knew that to be true still, even in the dream.
You'd been out – at work maybe? –
having a good day, almost energetic.

We seemed to be moving from some old house
where we'd lived, boxes everywhere, things
in disarray: that was the story of my dream,
but even asleep I was shocked out of the narrative

by your face, the physical fact of your face:
inches from mine, smooth-shaven, loving, alert.
Why so difficult, remembering the actual look
of you? Without a photograph, without strain?

So when I saw your unguarded, reliable face,
your unmistakable gaze opening all the warmth
and clarity of you – warm brown tea – we held
each other for the time the dream allowed.

Bless you. You came back, so I could see you
once more, plainly, so I could rest against you
without thinking this happiness lessened anything,
without thinking you were alive again.

Little bosom not yet cold

ALFRED, LORD TENNYSON

Little bosom not yet cold,
Nobel forehead made for thought,
Little hands of mighty mould
Clenched as in the fight which they had fought.
He had done battle to be born,
But some brute force of nature had prevailed
And the little warrior failed.
What'ere thou wert, what'ere thou art,

Whose life was ended ere their breath began,
Thou nine-months neighbour of my dear one's heart,
And howsoe'er thou liest blind and mute,
Thou lookest bold and resolute,
God bless thee dearest son.

Death is nothing at all [*extract*]

HENRY SCOTT HOLLAND

Death is nothing at all.
I have only slipped away to the next room.
I am I and you are you.
Whatever we were to each other,
That, we still are.

Call me by my old familiar name.
Speak to me in the easy way
which you always used.
Put no difference into your tone.
Wear no forced air of solemnity or sorrow.

Laugh as we always laughed
at the little jokes we enjoyed together.
Play, smile, think of me. Pray for me.
Let my name be ever the household word
that it always was.
Let it be spoken without effect.
Without the trace of a shadow on it.

Life means all that it ever meant.
It is the same that it ever was.
There is absolute unbroken continuity.
Why should I be out of mind
because I am out of sight?

I am but waiting for you.
For an interval.
Somewhere. Very near.
Just around the corner.

All is well.

Time flies

CHRISTINA ROSSETTI

Time flies, hope flags, life plies a wearied wing;
Death following hard on life gains ground apace;
Faith runs with each and rears an eager face,
Outruns the rest, makes light of everything,
Spurns earth, and still finds breath to pray and sing;
While love ahead of all uplifts his praise,
Still asks for grace and still gives thanks for grace,
Content with all day brings and night will bring.
Life wanes; and when love folds his wings above
Tired hope, and less we feel his conscious pulse,
Let us go fall asleep, dear friend, in peace:
A little while, and age and sorrow cease;
A little while, and life reborn annuls
Loss and decay and death, and all is love.

Auguries of Innocence [*extract*]

WILLIAM BLAKE

Man was made for joy and woe;
And when this we rightly know,
Through the world we safely go.
Joy and woe are woven fine,
A clothing for the soul divine.
Under every grief and pine
Runs a joy with silken twine.

Courage and inspiration

These are wise and wonderful poems about being open to possibility and change. Holub's simple piece 'The Door' asks us only to take a chance, to go and see what might be there if we take that small first step.

This chapter also includes poems about believing in yourself and offers reassurance that there is no right way to do something – trust yourself to take that step.

The Door

MIROSLAV HOLUB

Go and open the door.
　　Maybe outside there's
　　a tree, or a wood,
　　a garden,
　　or a magic city.

Go and open the door.
　　Maybe a dog's rummaging,
　　maybe you'll see a face,
　　or an eye,
　　or the picture
　　　　of a picture.

Go and open the door.
　　If there's a fog
　　it will clear.

Go and open the door.
　　Even if there's only
　　the darkness ticking,
　　even if there's only

the hollow wind,
even if
    nothing
       is there,
go and open the door.

At least
there'll be
a draught.

Entirely

LOUIS MACNEICE

If we could get the hang of it entirely
   It would take too long;
All we know is the splash of words in passing
   And falling twigs of song,
And when we try to eavesdrop on the great
   Presences it is rarely
That by a stroke of luck we can appropriate
   Even a phrase entirely.

If we could find our happiness entirely
 In somebody else's arms
We should not fear the spears of the spring nor the city's
 Yammering fire alarms
But, as it is, the spears each year go through
 Our flesh and almost hourly
Bell or siren banishes the blue
 Eyes of Love entirely.

And if the world were black or white entirely
 And all the charts were plain
Instead of a mad weir of tigerish waters,
 A prism of delight and pain,
We might be surer where we wished to go
 Or again we might be merely
Bored but in brute reality there is no
Road that is right entirely.

The Guest House

JALALUDDIN RUMI

This being human is a guest house.
Every morning a new arrival.

A joy, a depression, a meanness,
some momentary awareness comes
as an unexpected visitor.

Welcome and entertain them all!
Even if they're a crowd of sorrows,
who violently sweep your house
empty of its furniture,
still, treat each guest honourably.
He may be clearing you out
for some new delight.

The dark thought, the shame, the malice,
meet them at the door laughing,
and invite them in.

Be grateful for whoever comes,
because each has been sent
as a guide from beyond.

What if this road

SHEENAGH PUGH

What if this road, that has no held surprises
these many years, decided not to go
home after all; what if it could turn
left or right with no more ado
than a kite-tail? What if its tarry skin
were like a long, supple bolt of cloth,
that is shaken and rolled out, and takes
a new shape from the contours beneath?
And if it chose to lay itself down
in a new way; around a blind corner,
across hills you must climb without knowing
what's on the other side; who would not hanker
to be going, at all risks? Who wants to know
a story's end, or where a road will go?

Beauty

EDWARD THOMAS

What does it mean? Tired, angry, and ill at ease,
No man, woman, or child alive could please
Me now. And yet I almost dare to laugh
Because I sit and frame an epitaph –
'Here lies all that no one loved of him
And that loved no one.' Then in a trice that whim
Has wearied. But, though I am like a river
At fall of evening when it seems that never
Has the sun lighted it or warmed it, while
Cross breezes cut the surface to a file,
This heart, some fraction of me, happily
Floats through a window even now to a tree
Down in the misting, dim-lit, quiet vale;
Not like a pewit that returns to wail
For something it has lost, but like a dove
That slants unanswering to its home and love.
There I find my rest, and through the dusk air
Flies what yet lives in me. Beauty is there.

Small Boy

NORMAN MACCAIG

He picked up a pebble
and threw it into the sea.

And another, and another.
He couldn't stop.

He wasn't trying to fill the sea.
He wasn't trying to empty the beach.

He was just throwing away,
nothing else but.

Like a kitten playing
he was practicing for the future

when there'll be so many things
he'll want to throw away

if only his fingers will unclench
and let them go.

Variation on a Theme by Rilke

DENISE LEVERTOV

A certain day became a presence to me;
there it was, confronting me – a sky, air, light:
a being. And before it started to descend
from the height of noon, it leaned over
and struck my shoulder as if with
the flat of a sword, granting me
honour and a task. The day's blow
rang out, metallic – or it was I, a bell awakened,
and what I heard was my whole self
saying and singing what it knew: I can.

They don't publish the good news

THICH NHAT HANH

They don't publish
the good news.
The good news is published
by us.
We have a special edition every moment,

and we need you to read it.
The good news is that you are alive,
and the linden tree is still there,
standing firm in the harsh Winter.
The good news is that you have wonderful eyes
to touch the blue sky.
The good news is that your child is there before you,
and your arms are available:
hugging is possible.
They only print what is wrong.
Look at each of our special editions.
We always offer the things that are not wrong.
We want you to benefit from them
and help protect them.
The dandelion is there by the sidewalk,
smiling its wondrous smile,
singing the song of eternity.
Listen! You have ears that can hear it.
Bow your head.
Listen to it.
Leave behind the world of sorrow
and preoccupation
and get free.
The latest good news
is that you can do it.

Invictus

WILLIAM ERNEST HENLEY

Out of the night that covers me,
    Black as the Pit from pole to pole,
I thank whatever gods may be
    For my unconquerable soul.

In the fell clutch of circumstance
    I have not winced nor cried aloud.
Under the bludgeonings of chance
    My head is bloody, but unbowed.

Beyond this place of wrath and tears
    Looms but the Horror of the shade,
And yet the menace of the years
    Finds and shall find me unafraid.

It matters not how strait the gate,
    How charged with punishments the scroll,
I am the master of my fate,
    I am the captain of my soul.

A Journey

EDWARD FIELD

When he got up that morning everything was different:
He enjoyed the bright spring day
But he did not realize it exactly, he just enjoyed it.

And walking down the street to the railroad station
Past magnolia trees with dying flowers like old socks
It was a long time since he had breathed so simply.

Tears filled his eyes and it felt good
But he held them back
Because men didn't walk around crying in that town.

And waiting on the platform at the station
The fear came over him of something terrible about
    to happen:
The train was late and he recited the alphabet to keep
    hold.

And in its time it came screeching in
And as it went on making its usual stops,
People coming and going, telephone poles passing,

He hid his head behind a newspaper
No longer able to hold back the sobs, and willed his eyes
To follow the rational weavings of the seat fabric.

He didn't do anything violent as he had imagined.
He cried for a long time, but when he finally quieted
   down
A place in him that had been closed like a fist was open,

And at the end of the ride he stood up and got off that
   train:
And through the streets and in all the places he lived in
   later on
He walked, himself at last, a man among men,
With such radiance that everyone looked up and
   wondered.

HOPE

'... hope is the hardest
love we carry ...'

When we get out of bed each morning and
face the day it is easy to forget that we do
so because we have a sense of hope and an
idea of our own future to warm us and
drive us – something to aim for. Sometimes
this is so hard to find. These poems are
a mixture of those that understand how
difficult hope can be to keep and those that
are full of the stuff.

New Every Morning

SUSAN COOLIDGE

Every morning is a fresh beginning,
Listen my soul to the glad refrain.
And, spite of old sorrows
And older sinning,
Troubles forecasted
And possible pain,
Take heart with the day and begin again.

The Eclipse

RICHARD EBERHART

I stood out in the open cold
To see the essence of the eclipse
Which was its perfect darkness.

I stood in the cold on the porch
And could not think of anything so perfect
As man's hope of light in the face of darkness.

So Much Happiness

NAOMI SHIHAB NYE

It is difficult to know what to do with so much
   happiness.
With sadness there is something to rub against,
a wound to tend with lotion and cloth.
When the world falls in around you, you have pieces to
   pick up,
something to hold in your hands, like ticket stubs or
   change.

But happiness floats.
It doesn't need you to hold it down.
It doesn't need anything.
Happiness lands on the roof of the next house, singing,
and disappears when it wants to.
You are happy either way.
Even the fact that you once lived in a peaceful tree house
and now live over a quarry of noise and dust
cannot make you unhappy.
Everything has a life of its own,
it too could wake up filled with possibilities
of coffee cake and ripe peaches,

and love even the floor which needs to be swept,
the soiled linens and scratched records ...

Since there is no place large enough
to contain so much happiness,
you shrug, you raise your hands, and it flows out of you
into everything you touch. You are not responsible.
You take no credit, as the night sky takes no credit
for the moon, but continues to hold it, and to share it,
and in that way, be known.

Eternity

WILLIAM BLAKE

He who binds to himself a joy
Does the winged life destroy;
But he who kisses the joy as it flies
Lives in eternity's sunrise.

Evening

RAINER MARIA RILKE

Translated from the German by James Sheard

The evening slowly disrobes, and hands
each garment to a row of old attendant trees.
You look on, and watch how two worlds depart –
one heaven-bound, and one which falls,

and they leave you: to your not-quite-belonging
to either – not quite as dark as the silent house,
not quite so safely given up to eternity
as the thing that becomes a star and rises each night;

and they leave you (these threads cannot be untangled)
to your life, your timid, tall and growing life,
so that – at once limited and understood –
by turns a stone is grown in you, and then a star.

Instant Karma

ROY MARSHALL

The office cleaner sings beautifully and in Hindi.
I ask her what her song means.

'The Lord says, I will give you what you want,
when the time is right.'

She leaves a world bright with belief,
the mopped floor under my feet,

the emptied bin of me.

Hope and Love

JANE HIRSHFIELD

All winter
the blue heron
slept among the horses.
I do not know
the custom of herons,
do not know
if the solitary habit
is their way,
or if he listened for
some missing one –
not knowing even
that was what he did –
in the blowing
sounds in the dark.
I know that
hope is the hardest
love we carry.
He slept
with his long neck
folded, like a letter
put away.

Hope

EMILY DICKINSON

'Hope' is the thing with feathers
That perches in the soul,
And sings the tune without the words,
And never stops at all,

And sweetest in the gale is heard;
And sore must be the storm
That could abash the little bird
That kept so many warm.

I've heard it in the chillest land,
And on the strangest sea;
Yet, never, in extremity,
It asked a crumb of me.

If

RUDYARD KIPLING

If you can keep your head when all about you
    Are losing theirs and blaming it on you,
If you can trust yourself when all men doubt you,
    But make allowance for their doubting too;
If you can wait and not be tired by waiting,
    Or being lied about, don't deal in lies,
Or being hated, don't give way to hating,
    And yet don't look too good, nor talk too wise:

If you can dream – and not make dreams your master;
    If you can think – and not make thoughts
    your aim;
If you can meet with Triumph and Disaster
    And treat those two impostors just the same;
If you can bear to hear the truth you've spoken
    Twisted by knaves to make a trap for fools,
Or watch the things you gave your life to, broken,
    And stoop and build 'em up with worn-out tools:

If you can make one heap of all your winnings
    And risk it on one turn of pitch-and-toss,

And lose, and start again at your beginnings
    And never breathe a word about your loss;
If you can force your heart and nerve and sinew
    To serve your turn long after they are gone,
And so hold on when there is nothing in you
    Except the Will which says to them: 'Hold on!'

If you can talk with crowds and keep your virtue,
    Or walk with Kings – nor lose the common touch,
If neither foes nor loving friends can hurt you,
    If all men count with you, but none too much;
If you can fill the unforgiving minute
    With sixty seconds' worth of distance run,
Yours is the Earth and everything that's in it,
    And – which is more – you'll be a Man, my son!

TONICS TO LIFT THE SPIRITS

Be transported somewhere else with these poems: to the rolling countryside, a summer garden, the sea, to sit by a fire and look at snow or roses in the window, as Louis MacNeice recommends. What they all have in common is an uplifting instant of beauty and peace. Allow yourself to be whisked away and enjoy the moment of meditation and reflection.

Soon will the high Midsummer pomps come on

MATTHEW ARNOLD

Soon will the high Midsummer pomps come on,
    Soon will the musk carnations break and swell,
Soon shall we have gold-dusted snapdragon,
    Sweet-William with his homely cottage-smell,
       And stocks in fragrant blow;
Roses that down the alleys shine afar,
    And open, jasmine-muffled lattices,
    And groups under the dreaming garden-trees,
And the full moon, and the white evening-star.

Under Milk Wood [*extract*]

DYLAN THOMAS

Mary Anne Sailors dreams of
The Garden of Eden.
She comes in her smock-frock and clogs
away from the cool scrubbed cobbled kitchen
with the Sunday-school pictures on the
whitewashed wall and the farmers' almanac hung
above the settle and the sides of bacon on the
ceiling hooks, and goes down the cockleshelled
paths of that applepie kitchen garden, ducking
under the gippo's clothespegs, catching her apron
on the blackcurrant bushes, past beanrows and
onion-bed and tomatoes ripening on the wall
towards the old man playing the harmonium in
the orchard, and sits down on the grass at his side
and shells the green peas that grow up through the
lap of her frock that brushes the dew.

The Best Medicine

MEG COX

It must be genetic
that just lying on our backs
made me and my brother laugh.
When we had adjoining bedrooms
our mother would shout up the stairs
'stop reading now and go to sleep'.
Later she would shout again
'Stop laughing now'.

Adult, I went to yoga classes
and at the end we had to lie
on our backs on our mats and relax
doing yogic breathing, but before long
I was asked to leave before that part –
disruptive to meditation.

Come to think of it
lying on my back laughing
has caused me quite a bit of trouble
in the past.

Daffodils

WILLIAM WORDSWORTH

I wandered lonely as a cloud
That floats on high o'er vales and hills,
When all at once I saw a crowd,
A host, of golden daffodils;
Beside the lake, beneath the trees,
Fluttering and dancing in the breeze.

Continuous as the stars that shine
And twinkle on the milky way,
They stretched in never-ending line
Along the margin of a bay:
Ten thousand saw I at a glance,
Tossing their heads in sprightly dance.

The waves beside them danced; but they
Out-did the sparkling waves in glee:
A poet could not but be gay,
In such a jocund company:
I gazed – and gazed – but little thought
What wealth the show to me had brought:

For oft, when on my couch I lie
In vacant or in pensive mood,
They flash upon that inward eye
Which is the bliss of solitude;
And then my heart with pleasure fills,
And dances with the daffodils.

Pippa's Song

ROBERT BROWNING

The year's at the spring,
And day's at the morn;
Morning's at seven;
The hill-side's dew-pearl'd;
The lark's on the wing;
The snail's on the thorn;
God's in His heaven –
All's right with the world!

Advice Concerning Low Spirits

LETTER FROM SYDNEY SMITH TO LADY GEORGIANA
MORPETH, 16 FEBRUARY 1820

Dear Lady Georgiana,

Nobody has suffered more from low spirits than I have done – so I feel for you. 1st. Live as well as you dare. 2nd. Go into the shower-bath with a small quantity of water at a temperature low enough to give you a slight sensation of cold, 75° or 80°. 3rd. Amusing books. 4th. Short views of human life – not further than dinner or tea. 5th. Be as busy as you can. 6th. See as much as you can of those friends who respect and like you. 7th. And of those acquaintances who amuse you. 8th. Make no secret of low spirits to your friends, but talk of them freely – they are always worse for dignified concealment. 9th. Attend to the effects tea and coffee produce upon you. 10th. Compare your lot with that of other people. 11th. Don't expect too much from human life – a sorry business at the best. 12th. Avoid poetry, dramatic representations (except comedy), music, serious novels, melancholy, sentimental people, and everything likely to excite feeling or emotion, not ending in active benevolence. 13th. Do good, and endeavour to please everybody of every degree. 14th. Be as much as you can in the open air without fatigue. 15th. Make the room where you commonly sit, gay and pleasant. 16th. Struggle by little and little against idleness. 17th. Don't be too severe upon yourself, or underrate yourself, but do yourself justice. 18th. Keep good blazing fires. 19th. Be firm and constant in the exercise of rational religion. 20th. Believe me, dear Lady Georgiana,

Very truly yours,

Sydney Smith

Snow

LOUIS MACNEICE

The room was suddenly rich and the great bay-
    window was
Spawning snow and pink roses against it
Soundlessly collateral and incompatible:
World is suddener than we fancy it.

World is crazier and more of it than we think,
Incorrigibly plural. I peel and portion
A tangerine and spit the pips and feel
The drunkenness of things being various.

And the fire flames with a bubbling sound for world
Is more spiteful and gay than one supposes –
On the tongue on the eyes on the ears in the palms of
    your hands –
There is more than glass between the snow and the
    huge roses.

The Bright Field

R. S. THOMAS

I have seen the sun break through
to illuminate a small field
for a while, and gone my way
and forgotten it. But that was the pearl
of great price, the one field that had
treasure in it. I realize now
that I must give all that I have
to possess it. Life is not hurrying

on to a receding future, nor hankering after
an imagined past. It is the turning
aside like Moses to the miracle
of the lit bush, to a brightness
that seemed as transitory as your youth
once, but is the eternity that awaits you.

Under Milk Wood [*extract*]

DYLAN THOMAS

Herring gulls heckling down to the harbour
where the fishermen spit and prop the morning
up and eye the fishy sea smooth to the sea's end
as it lulls in blue. Green and gold money,
tobacco, tinned salmon, hats with feathers, pots
of fish-paste, warmth for the winter-to-be,
weave and leap in it rich and slippery in the
flash and shapes of fishes through the cold sea-streets.
But with blue lazy eyes the fishermen gaze at
that milkmild whispering water with no ruck or
ripple.

Loveliest of trees

A. E. HOUSMAN

Loveliest of trees, the cherry now
Is hung with bloom along the bough,
And stands about the woodland ride
Wearing white for Eastertide.

Now, of my threescore years and ten,
Twenty will not come again,
And take from seventy springs a score,
It only leaves me fifty more.

And since to look at things in bloom
Fifty springs are little room,
About the woodlands I will go
To see the cherry hung with snow.

Adlestrop

EDWARD THOMAS

Yes, I remember Adlestrop –
The name, because one afternoon
Of heat the express-train drew up there
Unwontedly. It was late June.

The steam hissed. Someone cleared his throat.
No one left and no one came
On the bare platform. What I saw
Was Adlestrop – only the name

And willows, willow-herb, and grass,
And meadowsweet, and haycocks dry,
No whit less still and lonely fair
Than the high cloudlets in the sky.

And for that minute a blackbird sang
Close by, and round him, mistier,
Farther and farther, all the birds
Of Oxfordshire and Gloucestershire.

Late Fragment

RAYMOND CARVER

And did you get what
you wanted from this life, even so?
I did.
And what did you want?
To call myself beloved, to feel myself
beloved on the earth.

Recommended reading

These are all poems that I regularly prescribe and wasn't able to include in this book. They are, at the time of going to press, available in print or online. I also sometimes prescribe whole poetry collections and anthologies, the best of which I've listed below.

For days when the world is too much with us

'I Am in Need of Music' by Elizabeth Bishop; 'Wild Geese' and 'Starlings in Winter' by Mary Oliver; 'Prayer' by Carol Anne Duffy.

Carpe diem

'The Summer Day' and 'The Journey' by Mary Oliver; 'Carpe Diem' by Robert Frost; 'What Do Women Want?' by Kim Addonizio; 'Vigil' by Dennis O'Driscoll.

Now I become myself

'For Desire' by Kim Addonizio; 'Lost' by David Wagoner; 'Warning' by Jenny Joseph; 'Danse Russe' by William Carlos Williams; 'If People Disapprove of You' by Sophie Hannah.

Love

'I Loved You' by Alexander Pushkin; 'Never Offer Your Heart to Someone Who Eats Hearts' and 'I'm Really Very Fond' by Alice Walker; 'The Retreat' by Charles Bukowski; 'Bloody Men' by Wendy Cope; 'Story of a Hotel Room' by Rosemary Tonks; 'Please Can I Have a Man' by Selima Hill; 'West Wind 2' by Mary Oliver; 'Misgivings' by William Matthews; 'Tonight I Can Write the Saddest Lines' by Pablo Neruda.

Getting older

'Here' by Grace Paley; 'Lore' by R. S. Thomas.

Specifically for dementia: 'Names' by Wendy Cope; 'Alzheimer's' by Bob Hicok; 'Have We Had Easter Yet?' by

Alison Pryde; 'Losing It' by Pamela Vincent.

Be alive every moment of your life

'Chemotherapy' and 'Too Heavy' by Julia Darling; 'Let Evening Come' and 'Otherwise' by Jane Kenyon; 'Lauds' by Malachi Black; 'Loss' by Jan Williams; 'When Death Comes' by Mary Oliver.

Talking to grief

'Funeral Blues' by W. H. Auden; 'Happiness' by Jane Kenyon; 'Wild Geese' by Mary Oliver; 'Climbing My Grandfather' by Andrew Waterhouse; 'And Death Shall Have No Dominion' by Dylan Thomas; 'Heaven to Be' by Sharon Olds.

Miscarriage and stillbirth: 'Comfort' and 'Into the Hour' by Elizabeth Jennings; 'i carry your heart with me' by E. E. Cummings.

Courage and inspiration

'The Journey' and 'Starlings in Winter' by Mary Oliver; 'Lost' by David Wagoner; 'Any Morning' by William Stafford; 'Prayer' by Carol Anne Duffy.

Hope

'Starlings in Winter' and 'Wild Geese' by Mary Oliver; 'Any Morning' by William Stafford; 'Prayer' by Carol Anne Duffy.

Anthologies

Astley, Neil (Ed.), *Being Alive, Staying Alive* and *Being Human*, Bloodaxe Books (2002; 2004; 2011) are all accessible and intelligent general poetry anthologies.

Astley, Neil (Ed.), *Do Not Go Gentle: Poems for funerals*, Bloodaxe Books (2003)

Barber, Laura, *Poems for Life*, Penguin Classics (2007)

Darling, Julia and Fuller, Cynthia (Eds), *The Poetry Cure*, Bloodaxe Books (2005) is for those living with their own or a loved one's illness, physical or mental.

Denny, John Andrew (Ed.), *Through Corridors of Light: Poems of consolation in time of illness*, Lion (2011)

Forbes, Peter (Ed.), *We Have Come Through: 100 Poems celebrating courage in overcoming depression and trauma*, Bloodaxe Books (2003)

Halliday, John (Ed.), *Don't Bring Me No Rocking Chair: Poems on Ageing*, Bloodaxe Books (2013)

In Memorium: Poems of Bereavement, Candlestick Press (2012)

Collections

Darling, Julia, *Apology for Absence*, Arc Publications (2004)

Kenyon, Jane, *Let Evening Come: Selected Poems*, Bloodaxe Books (2005)

Oliver, Mary, *New and Selected Poems*, Volume One, Beacon Press (2004)

Darling, Julia, *Sudden Collapses in Public Places*, Arc Publications (2003)

Acknowledgement

I'd like to say thank you to the following poets who have supported this project with their generosity and friendship: Pippa Little, Wendy Pratt, Roz Goddard, Roy Marshall, Char March, Meg Cox, Liz Lefroy and Steve Harrison.

Thank you to Jonathan Davidson at Writing West Midlands for your advice and encouragement for the idea of the Emergency Poet from its earliest days, for helping with an Arts Council grant application and for your poems.

Finally to my partner, poet James Sheard, for your beautiful translations of the Rilke poems, for your unfailing belief in me and the mad idea of the Emergency Poet, and for your love poem.

CREDITS

The author and publisher are grateful to the following for permission to use material that is in copyright:

Fleur Adcock: 'Kissing' from *Poems 1960-2000*. Reproduced with the permission of Bloodaxe Books.

Wendell Berry: 'The Peace of Wild Things' and 'To Know the Dark' copyright © 2012 by Wendell Berry, from *New Collected Poems*. Reprinted by permission of Counterpoint.

Elizabeth Bishop: 'One Art' from *Poems* by Elizabeth Bishop, published by Jonathan Cape. Reprinted by permission of The Random House Group Limited.

Edip Cansever: 'Table' from *Dirty August*, reprinted with the kind permission of Richard Tillinghast.

Raymond Carver: 'Late Fragment' from *All of Us: The Collected Poems* by Raymond Carver, published by Harvill Press. Reprinted by permission of The Random House Group Ltd.

Nina Cassian: 'Ordeal' from *The Penguin Book of Women*

Poems (Enitharmon Press, 2010), reprinted with the permission of Dr R. V. Bailey.

Elaine Feinstein: 'Getting Older' and 'Long Life' from *Collected Poems and Translations* (Carcanet, 2002), reprinted with the permission of Carcanet Press Limited.

Edward Field: 'The Journey', reprinted with the kind permission of the author.

Roz Goddard: 'Drawing Him at Fifty', reprinted with the kind permission of the author and the publisher, Nine Arches Press.

Kerry Hardie: 'What's Left' from *Selected Poems* (2011), by kind permission of the author and The Gallery Press, Loughcrew, Oldcastle, County Meath, Ireland.

Seamus Heaney: 'Postscript' from *Opened Ground* (Faber and Faber), reprinted with the permission of Faber and Faber Ltd.

Jane Hirshfield: 'Burlap Sack', 'Tree' and 'Hope and Love' from *Each Happiness Ringed by Lions: Selected Poems* (Bloodaxe Books, 2005). Reproduced with the permission of Bloodaxe Books.

Index of poets

Index of titles, first lines and notable lines

Titles of poems are in **bold** type, first lines are in roman type, and notable lines are in *italic* type. The articles 'A' and 'The' are ignored for sorting purposes.